This notebook belongs to:

_____

Published by Sunsmile Books 2019
ISBN 978-0-9951255-3-7
inspired by the You're Special, You're Wonderful
and You're a Star inspirational storybooks
© Leitaya Macale 2019

www.ingramcontent.com/pod-product-compliance
Lightning Source LLC
Chambersburg PA
CBHW070436010526
44118CB00014B/2073